# GROCERIES

NORA CLAIRE MILLER

Fonograf Editions
Portland, OR

First Edition, First Printing

FONO40

Published by Fonograf Editions
www.fonografeditions.com

Distributed by NYU Press
NYUPress.org

The manufacturer's authorized representative in the EU for prod-
uct safety is Mare Nostrum Group B.V., Mauritskade 21D, 1091 GC
Amsterdam, The Netherlands. Email: gpsr@mare-nostrum.co.uk.

[c|mp]

Fonograf Editions is a proud member of the Community
of Literary Magazines and Presses

ISBN: 978-1-964499-54-3
ISBN (ebook): 978-1-964499-56-7
LCCN: 2025931319

# GROCERIES

FONOGRAF EDITIONS

# CONTENTS

Galileo's grocery list from November 23, 1609 is an accidental poem about life on Earth.

> Lentils, white chickpeas, rice, raisins, spelt
> Sugar, pepper, cloves, cinnamon, spices, jams
> Soaps, oranges
> Two ivory combs
> Malvasia by Lords Sagredo
> Two artillery balls
> Organ pipe of tin
> German lenses, polished
> Have rock crystal polished
> Pieces of mirror
> Tripolitan, "spantia"
> The mirror-maker under the insignia of the Kmg
> Small iron tuning chisels made in the Calle delle
> Acque
> To haggle about iron bowls
> or to make them out of stone, or like the artillery balls
> Privilege for the vocabulary
> Iron plane

Like any good poem, this list has its mysteries—where do you buy "Privilege for the vocabulary"? how do you make iron bowls out of stone? and what in the world is "spantia"?

As for those artillery balls, Galileo used their immaculate spheres not for war, but for lens-grinding—to make a telescope.

—

Nora Claire Miller's *Groceries* is a book that lets us glimpse, as if through a reversed telescope, life on Earth from afar:

life on earth is a transcription of falling.

—

life on earth is a meaningful measure.
life on earth is a lot for the weather.

—

life on earth is

a giant pink cylinder

with salt on all sides

a hard little door

a grocery store

something for sure

life on earth is a hammer with nails

Even if you've never thought of human existence as a transcription of falling, Miller's depictions of life on earth may feel oddly familiar—or intimately strange. Not since *Tender Buttons* has a book so thoroughly defamiliarized the world *tout court*. It's worth keeping in mind, as you read *Groceries*, that the central section of *Tender Buttons* is titled "Food."

—

"Bruised beans, two modii, chickens, twenty, a hundred apples, if you can find nice ones, a hundred or two hundred eggs, if they are for sale there at a fair price."

Roman soldiers stationed along Hadrian's wall sent out a slave for groceries one day in the first century CE. We still have bits and pieces of their imperial Door Dash list:

"8 sextarii of fish-sauce ... a modius of olives ..."

—

Objects. Food. Rooms. *Tender Buttons* divides up the sensible world into three kinds of things. There's an uncanny tenderness to Miller's way of looking at things, or the *shape* of things, too:

a shape is proximal to its axes.

that is the beauty of shapes.

we can stand very still next to them.

This could be Euclid speaking, or Gertrude Stein, or a visitor from Mars. The beauty of shapes is mathematical, abstract, and alien. *Groceries* draws a silhouette of the world.

Another word for a shape is a form. Form is a word that's preoccupied poets since time immemorial. The shapes that proliferate throughout Miller's art make form new. Not only literary form, but that, too.

Maybe it's a form of alienation, or the form of their alienation that makes me feel like a citizen in Miller's alien nation:

> I'm not real, but shapes are real.
> but I'm not shapes, but I'm not a forest of shapes.
> not magnets. not hornets. glass bugs.
> and it wasn't as if a wasp, so much as it
> was a wasp, and a wasp was a noun.
> this was what I told myself, at least,
> as I washed my hands.

—

There are all sorts of things in Miller's inventory of life on earth. Magnets, hornets, glass bugs, a wasp, daffodils, horses, violets of many colors—the list goes on.

And there are unfathomable mysteries in *Groceries*, too. They take the shape of boxes, lots of little boxes, or squares, or maybe cursors—I'm not sure what to do with them, or make of them, but I think I can recognize them:

> on earth there are a lot of patterns ( ☐ ☐☐ ☐☐☐ ☐ ☐☐ ☐☐☐…). on earth there are a lot of people who think they can recognize patterns ( ☐☐☐☐☐☐☐).

Maybe they're only characters—typographical characters, like the ones you're reading now. But that doesn't mean they don't mean anything: "if you pick the wrong ☐," Miller writes, or types, "the ☐ will erupt."

—

"Send me a shirt, towel, trousers, reins, and, for my sister, send fabric."

In Medieval Russia, a father once signed off a shopping list for his son—

"If I am alive, I will pay for it."

—

What will the world look like when it ends? An empty box, I guess:

> there will be no more gardenias or sunglasses or mops or apostrophes or natural disasters. there will be no more latex-free gloves or endeavors or external hard drives. there will be no more lie detector tests or astonishing new pieces of information. there will be no more guilt. there will be no more admonitions.

I'd miss the gardenias and the astonishing new pieces of information. The natural disasters, external hard drives, and admonitions, not so much. Miller isn't sentimental about life on earth—but they aren't heartless about it either.

—

Galileo Galilei is nowhere to be found in Miller's book. You won't find any ancient Roman soldiers here, or Medieval Russian fathers, either. But *Groceries* belongs on our list of inventories for eternity.

—

Is life on earth a thing—a condition of existence, a collective historical narrative, a population?

Or is life on earth a form—a social practice, a set of customs, a kind of ceremony?

Maybe life on earth, this poet shows us, is simply something to be addressed:

> life on earth, oh my god life on earth. I don't know who you are or where I heard your name before, but I must have heard of you, life on earth.

so I became unrealistic and thought of days
of how life on earth was a vanishing experiment
in deciding or pointer fingers, as the videos
next door yell into their beers or their cooking,
LIFE ON EARTH IS INTOLERABLE! so acting
becomes dangerous, as does cooking, each of us making
our own omelets, in our own apartments,
every sunday, here on earth. they say life on earth
is a big disappointment. but I can tell you
all the teeth I have: incisor. incisor. premolar. incisor.
molar. premolar. molar. incisor. molar. premolar.
incisor. premolar. premolar. canine. canine.
incisor. molar. incisor. premolar. canine. molar. molar.
molar. premolar. molar. incisor. premolar. canine.

life on earth is

a giant pink cylinder

with salt on all sides

a hard little door

a grocery store

something for sure

on earth, I walk by □□□　　　　□　□　□　　　　□　□　　　□

□ light switches □　　□

□　　　　　　□□

□　□　□　□　　mechanical　pencils　　□　□　□　□

□□□　□□□　□　□□□　　　　　　□　□　□

□　automated　alerts　　□　□　□　□　□　□　　　□　□　□　□

□□□□□　□□□□□　□□　□　□　　□　□　□　□

□□□　□□

□□□　□　　　□□　　□□□□

]　□□□　　　□□□□□□□□□□□□□□□□□□□□□□□□□　rubber　spatulas □□□□□

□□□□□　□□□□□□　□□□　□□□　□　□　□□□

　　　　　□　□　□　□　□　□

□　□　□　□　□　□　□　□□　□　□□□　□□□□　□　□　□　　□　　　□[

□　□　□　□□　□□　□□□□　　□

finally, I arrive at the shore to watch the river leak. some
guy comes up and tries to kick me out. you can't kick me
out of here, I say to him, but he kicks me out anyway. as I
leave, I look at all the buildings made of □not containing
anything

the future is firm about ⬚s.

some are thoroughfares,

while others are simply for decoration.

if you pick the wrong ⬚,

the ⬚ will erupt.

⬚

you tell them.

⬚

no, you.

⬚

I am only

here for a little while.

there will be no more gardenias or sunglasses or mops or apostrophes or natural disasters. there will be no more latex-free gloves or endeavors or external hard drives. there will be no more lie detector tests or astonishing new pieces of information. there will be no more guilt. there will be no more admonitions.

a university is not a television station. a university is not a circle you can walk around. a university is not a telephone or a table lamp or a table. a university is just a plot device.

cooking is not what it is supposed to be. cooking cannot do what it is supposed to do. when you direct a university at cooking the university will be cooked or the cooking will be universalized but nobody will ever learn anything. it is a growing problem and there will be a panel discussion.

information is to a room as yelling is to stationary. yelling is to a room, as is a university. when a university looks, you can be called. we will endeavor to respond.

it felt like every person in the video was swimming.

a person was swimming. a video was swimming.

a person in a video was swimming

and the remote controls were growing out of the water.

it was like everyone in the video was being sewn

or standing next to someone who was sewing.

an organization is not a task that can be accomplished.

a task is a task that takes no time

but offers every solution.

a shape is proximal to its axes.

that is the beauty of shapes.

we can stand very still next to them.

there's still time to iron a perfect hem,

to press the daffodils carefully into the kitchen sink with water,

to show other people how to speak to horses.

you do it mostly with your eyes and ears.

you do it mostly while standing at a distance.

when it rains at a university it is an indoor sort of rain.

that is to say, it makes the shape of rain without actually raining.

on earth there is not only good (□□□) and bad (□□), but also particle-board (□□□□□), microsoft word (□□□□□), motion-detecting lights (□　□　□　□□□□□), analogies (□□□　□□　□□). on earth there is no real accomplishment in purchasing (□□　□), scoring (□□□), or deciding (□□□□). these things are simply signs of pattern recognition. on earth there are a lot of patterns (□□□□　□□□　□　□□…). on earth there are a lot of people who think they can recognize patterns (□□□□).

I am challenged by an abstract public art piece. it attacks me unprovoked. excuse me, I say, squinting upward at its metal figure in the sun. it curses me with its eyes. we start to do battle. I hold the upper hand because I am not a statue. the fight goes on awhile. when we are finished, we are somehow indoors.

□　　□　　　□　□□□ □where's a good place
　　　□□□ □□□□□for cloud computing?

　　　I wanted to talk about □□ □□ □□ □□
　　　　　　　　　　　□□ □□


　　　　　　　　　　　　　the electrical grid　□ □□　□ □□　　　□
　　　　　　　　　　□　　　　　　□□
　　　　　　　□　　　　　　□□　　　　　□
a container of water　□　□□　　　□□
　　　　　　　□　　　□
　　　　　□
　　　　　　　　□

analysis

□□ □□□□
□□□□□ □□□□□　later　　　□□□□□

　　　　　　　　　　　　　　canned soup

　　　　　　　　　　　　　□ □

rabbit hair
□　　　　　□　　　　　　　　　□
　　　　　　　　□　　　　□
□ □ □ □□□　　　　　　　　□　　　□　　　+
bound only by joy

　　　　　　　　　□□□ my electric bill □□□
when I was　□ □□ finished recording　□□□□□□□□ □□ □
　　　　　　□□□□□□□
　　　　　　　　　　　　□ □　　　□ □
　　　　　　　　　　　I began to hang up

13

after a while, I finished reading and began to leave the park. it was night on the outskirts of the diorama, and everyone was drinking from empty beers and asking questions about the weather. what was it made out of, what did it want, etc. suddenly, one man started shouting from inside the diorama. "THE ELECTRIC BILL COMES FROM WITHIN YOU."

□ □ □ □ □ □ □ □ □ □ □ □ □

□ □ □ □ □ □ □ □□ □ □ □ □ □ □ □□

□ □ □ □ □ □ □ □

□ □ □ □ □ □ □□□ □ □ □ □

 I had finished recording my voicemail, so I just hung up the phone after he said it. then I watched as, like power does, he disappeared. it was morning in the electrical city, the one that only existed inside a tiny piece of glass in my pocket and some warehouses several hundred miles away.

□ □ □ □ □ □ □ □ □ □

□ □ □ □ □ □ □ □ □ □ □ □ □ □

□ □ □ □ □ □ □ □ □ □

□ □ □ □ □ □ □ □ □ □□ □ □ □ □ □□

□□□□□□□ □□□□□□ □ □ □ □ □ □□

□□□□□□□□□□

□

□□□□□□□ □ □ □□

□□□□ □ □

□ □

□ □ □ □ □ □ □

□□ □ □ □ □ □□□ □

□ □ □ □ □

□ □ □ □ □ □□ □□          □□□□□□ □□ □□□□□□□ □

□          □          □ □□          □□□□□□□ □□

□□                    □□□□□ □

□□□□□□                    □

in the streets which were bathed in swathes of digital sun,
I walked my electric cat on a leash. she was learning about
her world, smelling the surging drainpipes of buildings,
the pixelated sequences of isometric sand that lined the
gutters, when all of a sudden we ran into a man.

□□□   □□

□□□□          □          □          □□□□□□□□□

□                    □                    □          □

□

☐ ☐ ☐☐ ☐☐☐☐☐☐☐☐☐☐ ☐☐☐ ☐☐☐☐☐☐☐☐☐☐☐☐ ☐

☐☐☐☐☐☐☐☐☐☐☐☐ ☐☐☐☐☐☐☐☐☐☐ ☐☐☐☐☐☐☐☐☐☐☐ ☐☐☐☐

☐☐☐☐☐☐☐ ☐☐"fancy some garnishes?" ☐ ☐ ☐ ☐ ☐

he asked, and without ☐ ☐☐☐☐☐☐☐☐☐☐☐ ☐☐☐ ☐☐☐☐

waiting for response thrust several jars ☐ ☐ ☐☐☐☐☐☐☐ [

☐☐☐☐ ☐☐☐☐ ☐☐☐☐of vegetables—pickled-looking,

☐ ☐☐☐☐☐☐☐☐☐☐☐ ☐☐☐ ☐☐☐☐wretched—into

my hands. without thinking, I reached, reflexively, ☐

☐☐☐☐☐☐☐☐☐☐☐ ☐☐☐ ☐☐☐☐to grasp them. ☐ ☐☐☐

☐☐☐☐☐☐☐ ☐☐☐ ☐☐☐☐☐☐ holding the jars felt

like touching the ☐ ☐☐☐☐☐☐☐☐☐☐☐ ☐☐☐ ☐☐☐☐

underside of an anthill. ☐☐☐☐☐☐☐ ☐☐☐☐☐☐☐☐☐☐

☐☐☐ ☐☐☐ ☐☐☐☐☐☐☐☐☐☐☐ ☐☐☐☐☐☐☐☐☐☐☐ ☐☐☐☐ ☐ ☐ ☐ ☐☐ [

☐☐☐☐☐☐☐☐ ☐☐☐☐☐☐☐☐☐☐☐☐ ☐☐☐☐☐☐☐☐☐☐

☐ ☐☐☐☐ ☐☐☐☐☐☐☐☐☐☐ ☐☐☐ ☐☐☐☐ ☐☐☐ ☐ ☐

17

I wondered for a long time as we stood there about the secret truth about the jars. finally, I asked him. "what is the secret truth about the jars?" he looked at me and then at the cat. then he began to embroider little flowers on the sidewalk.

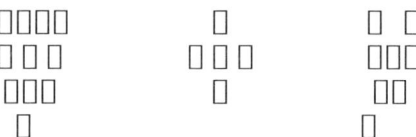

I'd had enough of him and wanted to stop talking. I wasn't the only one. but after a while, his phone started to ring. it rang so much it started raining a little. it was clear that whoever was calling was not going to give up.

I wasn't sure

what we were

going to do

when the calls stopped          coming in

when the

weather was all gone

the electric bill would be gone,

then, too

□　□　　□　□　　□　□　　　　　□but the weather was far □□

　　　□□□□　　　　□□□□□□□　　　　　□□□□□

　　　□□□　　□□□□□

　　　□□□□□□□□□□□□□□□□□□from over □　□　　□

　　　　　□□□　□□

　　　　　　□　　　　□□□　　　　　□□□□□□□□

　　□□□□□□□□□□□□

　　　　　□□

　　□□　□　□□□□　　　　the liquids had their containers □□□

□

the men had their dioramas □□□□　　□□　　□　□　□□

　　□　　　□□□

　　□　　　□　　　□□□□□□　　□□　　□　　　□□□

　　　　□□□

　　　　　　　the thunder had already started

　　　□□□□　　　　□□□□□□□　□□　　　　　　□□

　　　　□□□□□

　　　　　　by the time we noticed the　□s in the sky

　　□□　　　□　　　□□　□□□　　　□　　　□□□□　□□

　　□

　　　□□□　□　　　　□□□　□　　　□□□□

　　　□□□□□□□　　　□

　　　　　　□　　　　　　□□□

　　　　　□□□

　　□　　　　　　　　□　　　　　　　　　□□□□□□　□　□　　　□

on earth there is a photograph of earth
and a photograph of jupiter and a photograph
of tonsillitis. it feels like a big inhale.
it feels like getting in trouble, but oh, how the stars
do gleam, how the mountaintops do tremble.
this is all well and good. but a photograph
is not a photograph at all, just an expression
of light. it's an aerial view: pull over
to the shoulder of grief, pay a visit
to the airplane hanger of grief, go live online
in a city named for grief. on earth everything changes,
horses lunge, straight people flirt with their bannisters,
the rest of us make overhead shapes.
on earth the weather gets worse,
it makes us so frantic, people start to construct notions:
sweaters and gelatin molds. fruits and vegetables.
smoke alarms go off again next door.
you can call them whatever you want
but there will always be horses.
on earth there are many words for horses.

are they playing or pausing?　　□□□　□

　　　　　　　　　　□　□　　□


are they standing still or not really?

　　　　　　　□□ □□

　　　　　　　　□□□ □□□□ □□□□□

　　　　　　　　　　never dividing, never diving,

　　　　　　　□□□□　□□□□□□□□

　　　　　　　　□□□□□


　□ □ □ □ □ □ □ □ □ □ □ □ □

　□ □ □ □ □ □ □ □ □ □ □ □ □

　□ □ never washing myself in sunlight, □

　□ □ □ □ □ □ □ □ □ □ □ □ □

　□ □ □ □ □ □ □ □ □ never eliding,

I was born to be gigantic,

said the violet flower that derailed me.

this is a rumor, so there aren't

any rules to go with it. I built its shape of pegs,

won't take that lying down, my name is zero,

my name is nonce, my name is nobody, who the hell are you.

yesterday I tried to buy a joke.

I brought it to my home,

took it inside slowly like how you

come out of a bath. there was nothing new

to say about it. to make the violet speak to you,

just go crazy, said my second-grade art teacher

handing me construction paper, glue.

just go crazy, I say now to the flower,

engulfed as I was by her lesson. her lesson to

say more plainly the visual field. to draw to

the lowermost quadrant of the paper.

to draw upon my limits like ribbons of gas,

to "make these limits assets"

(to write about them in essays).

to see the ending from both sides,

so profound was my derailment.

I walk into the grocery store. the mood is historic, the scene is destructive. I expect the potato-haired woman to offer me a sample. instead, she begins to sing right there in the aisle:

life on earth is fragile.
life on earth is frugal.
life on earth is furtive.
life on earth is futuristic.

life on earth, oh my god life on earth. I don't know who you are or where I heard your name before, but I must have heard of you, life on earth.

if the causing were spinning faster.

if the cereal came from thin air.

if I had to think of bereavement.

if I weren't such a coward

and could visit the billing website

during normal business hours.

if the cereal tasted different because it was generic.

if I used more nouns.

if I had to think of sunshine.

if I opened my socks like thin little books

if I hid everything that could be seen, what would knowing be.

a basket. a signal of time: it just sways. it just stops.

miracle: a row of tulips pointing down,

beneath a structure shaped like an armoire,

hurtling through space, not outer space exactly.

the tulips jagged like teeth. the colors

behind them complimentary yet brash.

a feeling of vastness. there are places

where the ☐ goes dead.

if only life on earth could be made

into oatmeal, you'd eat it every morning,

and perhaps one day grow larger than it,

like a book whose pages have swelled permanently

open after a flood. dried out, askance, wafer-like.

frightful how its faces gleam, how the vines grow

together on the shelf above. in the sky, the airplanes

start to hurt, they start to come down,

they're falling like rain

coins in a beautiful grid! floating!

coins! in action! coming! going!

coins! arranged! comfortably! floating!

coins! in the accurate knowing!

□□　　□□　　□□
□□　　□□　　□□
□□　　□□　　□□
□□　　□□　　□□
□□　　□□　　□□
□□　　□□　　□□
□□　　□□　　□□
□□　　□□　　□□
□□　　□□　　□□
□□　　□□　　□□
□□　　□□　　□□
□□　　□□　　□□
□□　　□□　　□□
□□　　□□　　□□
□□　　□□　　□□
□□　　□□　　□□
□□　　□□　　□□
□　　□□　　□□　　□□　　□　□　□　　□　□
　　□　　　□　　　□　　□
□　　□　　□　　□　　we made numbers
and associated each of them with an object. this went
well, but when it was over, we didn't know where
to put the numbers that went with the objects. we
knew where to put the objects on their own, and we
knew where to put the numbers on their own, but
combining them? impossible. □□　　　□　　　□□
□□　　□□　　□□　　□　□　□□　　□□
□□　　□　□　　□□　　□□　　□□　　□□
　　□　　　□　　　□

□　　　□ □　　□ □　　□ □　　□　　□　　□　　□

　　　　□　　　　□　　　　□

□　　　　□　　　　□　　　　□　　　　□ □　　　□ □ □ □

□

□ □ □ □ □ □　　　　　　　　　　□　　　　　□ □ □ □

we glued a few of the numbers to the window above the
kitchen sink. we tacked some other numbers behind
the curtains and some other numbers went into a folder
called "the numbers."

　　□　□　　□　□

□　　　　□　　　　□　　　　□　　　　□　　　　□　　　　□

　□　□　□　　　□　□

this went well, but when we were finished distributing
the numbers we didn't know who any of our friends
were, □or where to find them, or their names.

□ □　　　　□　　　　□　　　　□　　　　□　　　□ □

□ □ □　□ □ □ □　　□　　　　□　　　　□　　　　□　　□ □

　　□　□　　　　□　　　　□　　　　□

□ □ □　□　　　　□　　　　□　　　　□

□ □ □　□　　　　　　　□　　　　□　　　　□　　　□

　　　　　　　　□　　　　□　　　　□

　　　　　　　　□　　　　□　　　　□

　　　　　　　　□　　　　□　　　　□

　　　　　　　　□　　　　□　　　　□

　　　　　　　　□　　　　□　　　　□

　　　　　　　　□　　　　□　　　　□

　　　　　　　　□　　　　□　　　　□

　　　　　　　　□　　　　□　　　　□

　　　　　　　　□　　　　□　　　　□

29

□□□
□□□
□□□
□□□
□□□
□□□ □
□□□ □□　　　□　　　□　　　□
□□□ □　　　□　　　□　　　□
□□□ □
　　　□□□□□　　　□□　　□　　□
□　　□　　□　　□　　□□　　□□　　□□
□　　□
□　　□　　□　　□

we looked for our friends on the phone, in the sky, by
helicopter, by signal light.

□□　　　　　　　　　　　　　　□□□
　　□□□□□

when we had finished, we made phone calls to each
object as previously scheduled.

　□□

these calls extended into the future.

how far into the future,

□□　　□　　□　　□　　□　　□　　□
□□□　□□

everybody wanted to know. there wasn't a clear answer.

the future was so unperturbed.

□□□　　　　　　　　　　　　　□□□□
　　　□□□□

□　　□　　□　　□□　　□□
□□□□　　　　□□□□
　　　　　□□　　　　　　　　□

30

I never was yelling on purpose.

I try to make shapes out of it. this

is one [],                  this is the other [].

the two can                 talk to each other

but only about              ice water and melting.

the shape in the            middle of it: that is

the shape. that is the shape of it.

in the next world, there will be no telling or talking or cereal or being upside down or outdoor sculptures to climb up on or hills to roll down or stretches of hot highway that turn to liquid at the horizon or instructions or proofreading jobs or ficus plants or figure skaters or cumulonimbus clouds or staring contests or zero-calorie sugar substitutes or heart-shaped sunglasses or telephones.

but our cat Ramona

is standing in the next

world. but our cat Ramona

is standing in this world,

on this table, saying

TALK TO ME, NOTICE ME,

ANYBODY. but our cat Ramona

is not noticed, not talked to,

not by you, not by me,

not by anybody.

that is because to our cat

Ramona, sounds are not sounds

and noticing is not noticing.

it is only to us that

recognition is a blue

and green alarm clock,

an almond festival,

an arrow pointing up.

thus, though we often

address her directly,

we will never fully

notice our cat Ramona.

today I have not been in a grocery store but I am saying yes to everything. in the movie *the martian* the protagonist, matt damon, is stuck in outer space. he harvests potatoes grown in his own shit. his fellow astronauts leave him on mars. he makes a go of it anyway. there is no use describing the room I am in now, a room that is not a grocery store. matt damon's friends come back to mars to try and rescue him. and then what happens. matt damon dies. it's easier than you think.

□ □□□□　□　□□　□

staying still on soap avenue watching

the rugs disassemble beneath me.

□ □□□ □□ □ □□ □ □ □□□ □

first goes the rug, then goes the fiction,

1.　　□□ □□□ □ □
2.　　□ □ □ □ □

or so

the saying goes.

( □ □ □)

the saying goes,

(􀀀 􀀀 􀀀),

                                        rubber + oranges

                              􀀀 􀀀􀀀    􀀀    􀀀 􀀀 􀀀 􀀀

􀀀

+ roadside assistance

􀀀   􀀀􀀀                    􀀀􀀀􀀀

+ the whole piano  􀀀􀀀􀀀 􀀀􀀀 􀀀􀀀􀀀􀀀

                              􀀀􀀀􀀀􀀀

                                    + next sunday

                              􀀀

                                    􀀀

I step outside

to feel the joints

in the metallic trees.

the sky a giant comb

here on earth, or so

(􀀀 􀀀 􀀀)

rubber or dry fish or softness or hermit crabs. weather or leather or clotheslines. phosphorescent wristwatches, noises in the morass. or clotheslines. or morass. or pouring apple cider, facing away from the air conditioner, hair standing up against the vertical angle, television says stop what you're doing and I can't hear you and you're stepping out to the edge of the sky, you're starting on the bathroom sink, you're small, you're really tiny, you could read it or reach it, the mirror is tubing, the elevator hums, life on earth is a fucking disaster, life on earth is a hammer with nails,

soft gels

established practices

neighborhood cats

fruit roll-ups

goldman sachs

creamsicles

rubber flooring

soda bread

mushroom clouds

pencil erasers

bowling pins

been my name

curtain rods

the way to keep

going in

cellophane

antarctica

should have

cellophane

mister

if the cereal was generic!

if generic were even a part of it!

in the store everything is in buckets!

organic! semi-organic!

organic but wrapped in thick plastic!

in the grocery store things are changing!

nothing visible left in this aisle!

in this aisle or in the next aisle!

in that aisle or the next aisle!

microsoft word has such

beauty and permanence.

microsoft word has changed

my life. the point of microsoft word

is that you're alone. was there ever

anything better. a metallic color

is a color that appears to be

that of a polished metal.

the visual sensation associated

cannot be reproduced.

your fridge knows a lot of things about you. but do you know anything about your fridge. did you know. for example. that a fridge cannot get old. especially if it is clean. and a fridge cannot get cleaned. especially if it is old. a fridge can hear about you. a fridge can talk about you too. a fridge can ruin your life. and a fridge can breathe. a fridge can write a letter. and a fridge can litter. a fridge can get angry. and a fridge can listen.

having the wherewithal to go via helicopter.

wearing a lamp on your head or your shoulder.

life on earth is a meaningful measure.

life on earth is a lot for the weather.

if speech could be

dilated would it

scatter inside me

if I see beaches

would I stop to sit down

life on earth asks a lot

of tubes and wires

life on earth asks

me still but

I'm not tired

the future ships

separately, with a plastic

bag full of screws.

then again, ziploc

is not a word, it is a word

that was resolved.

any invention is a word

except for ziploc,

ziploc is an absolute.

this is vinyl.

do not burn it.

do not throw it away.

this is an elevator.

do not burn it.

if you talk to a  ▯

weather will come out.

no, no everyone

said so, no.

yes, you're not

responsible

for it, no. go

back inside,

go back inside, go.

every night I talk to my other selves from prior nights. we meet in the bathroom. we call ourselves "the night club." "hi, night club," we say to each other in passing, in the bathroom, late at night. the vent fan exhaling in the background. "life on earth sure is miserable, huh," we say to each other. we are all writing the same book, it is an inside joke. I remember spooning peanut butter in the kitchen at a job. the air outside was warm and the peanut butter was in an industrial-sized bucket, not the huge kind but the medium-sized kind, and I was scraping out the peanut butter and it got all over my arms and all over the medium-sized industrial-sized bucket. I didn't know which to wash first. all night, the earth folding in on itself, like mud.

life on earth isn't easy, though, buster. what drinks from a straw comes back to me as gold. again, say TOMATO SANDWICH. I don't want to. TOMATO SANDWICH. I don't have to. all right, TOMATO SANDWICH, I said, and then everything dropped off. I wanted to know, I mean I wanted to really know, what deciding was all about. even though no one asked me to know. even though I opened a document and said tell me how you want to die, and someone emailed back, I want to fall off a clocktower, I want to be rescued via helicopter, my ideal death is one I am saved from just in the nick of time. we can definitely put that in an essay and get you into medical school, I assure her. out the window, the sound of loons hitting propellers.

advice:

your website

should be a dot com

it should wear an antenna

an onion or lantern

it should ask you no questions

(real or imagined)

it should be an address

you should do what I'm asking

     ⬜learning to tell time ⬜

⬜learning to tell ⬜time learning ⬜

    ⬜to tell time ⬜learning to ⬜tell time ⬜

⬜learning ⬜to tell ⬜time ⬜learning ⬜

    ⬜to ⬜tell ⬜time ⬜then what ⬜is daylight

⬜savings ⬜time ⬜what does it ⬜mean ⬜

  ⬜who wants ⬜it to happen or ⬜decides ⬜

of course it was not spinning any faster.

of course no air could get out of it.

of course it was the wrong way to handle the situation,

mouth full of bubbles, room full of paint.

if it were a vehicle I would say, this car cannot be moved.

if it were a TV show I would rate it a zero and move on.

if it were a cast iron skillet I would say, douse the whole thing

in lye, scrub off the seasoning and start over.

if it were a horse, I would say, poor horse, you have not been

given a fair shake in life and now you are miserable and alone.

if it were a bucket of water I would want to drown in it.

if it were a cup of lemonade I would not ask for it.

if it were a laundry day it would be the symbol for laundry and

the symbol for day but there would be nothing to wash

and nowhere to sit.

if I could say it could I not also sit in it.

if I could see it. could

make it move with my eyes.

or if it grew sideways.

if I could only go near it.

the book says time
past time is still time,
except when it's not
written down. I say
time is a book past time,
except when the rest
is on purpose. in a book
about time, nothing had
better be written,
or ceded, or songed.
I wanted to be left alone.
okay, I will leave you alone.
honest, I'll leave you alone.

details exist. I'll loan you one. there's a book about talking to whales. I never read it. people say aquariums are for losers but I don't know. it's nice to go in. it's nice to categorize things: shape, shape, sound, shape, mixture. fish are easy and starfish are harder. echoes are the worst. when I open my umbrella and set out for someplace new, the ⬚s start talking. you're so out of touch, they tell me. but fixtures are just places to go back to.

life on earth is a transcription of falling.

you don't get to ask any questions

of the mercury thermometer, and you

still have to stand upon the top

of the hill, your knees rotating,

your face pointing down, the word

emergency stated calmly over an intercom,

warm grass, soda in a frosted glass,

slight smell of blood or detergent,

perfect like the number three

gulls can be shorthand.

gulfs can be longer.

can't talk right now,

in a fight with a flower.

in the airspace of calling.

don't come for my food.

it changes the meaning.

when someone says stop.

says there is no room.

I'm not hungry,

I said. doesn't matter.

a letter is like an olive except then what.

when bad things happen to good people

everyone says monopoly money, monopoly money,

get out the landing gulls, outstanding gulls.

I'm sorry. I meant to say.

the alphabets announce themselves.

new updates ready to be installed.

oh microsoft word, bring me to my knees.

on earth update later. on earth

restart app. on earth the letters

hum and slow and wheeze.

boots! in the household! boots! arrayed!

boots! like lampshades! on! display!

boots! hungry! tired! frayed!

boots! destroyed! then re! conveyed!

get in the honda. we're going to the coral ridge mall. the cats are coming too. come on. we're going motoring. something's almost done.　□ □　　□　　□　　　　　it's steaming like oatmeal.　　　　　□ □ □　□　□ □　　　it's in the middle images,　□　　　□　　　□　　　pouring forth from the cracks　□ □ □　　□ □ □　　　in the floor. a pitcher full of oranges. oh teach me to be an oval, to fill in until the circles return.

on earth, day breaks.

the clocks on the wall crack and rattle.

inside, you check your watch.

"IT IS THE ZERO HOUR."

that can't be accurate. you check again.

"WELCOME TO YESTERDAY, SUCKER."

that seems truer to reality.

you go make megaphones.

the rest of the day is unimportant.

"I'm here to buy groceries," I announce. a hush fills the room like grease.

at self checkout, the machine fills my bag with blue and gray □s just as I ask. I carry them around all day and ask questions:

"what do you delineate? what do you want to be? what do you think of my website?"

the □s answer,

"□ □ □                   □□□□□□□□
□□   □   □□                        □
□□□□□□ □ □□□□□ □   □                □□□
□ □ □ □ □□□□□ □                □□□□□
□ □□□ □  □□□□ □              □□,"

and then leave, not awaiting reply.

life on earth I shouldn't stop you I shouldn't forget you

life on earth I shouldn't catch you I shouldn't be inside you

life on earth is a cable or a muzzle

I could stop time to get there quicker

I could be right above you

ISO: a hungrier material.

more dimensional.

see-thru. a violet robe.

a hasty lobe.

a brilliant globe.

I'm not real, but shapes are real.
but I'm not shapes, but I'm not a forest of shapes.
not magnets. not hornets. glass bugs.
and it wasn't as if a wasp, so much as it
was a wasp, and a wasp was a noun.
this was what I told myself, at least,
as I washed my hands. as I washed my
hands, green and blue liquid exited
them and began interacting with the
porcelain of the sink. it started to
be stained green, and everyone was
upset about it, because there wasn't any place
to put the color green, so we rubbed it
on our clothing, which began to become
that green, or else a darker shade of green,
depending on the material to which it was applied.
no problem, I said, I will just buy another coat of paint
and place it on the outside of the porcelain of the sink.
this seemed well-reasoned at the time,
though later on, I began to regret it.
shapes were megaphones. worcestershire sauce.
flames. violet jets scraping the sky.
nothing could be wrung from any of our sentences.
we put them out on the deck to sun like magnets.

life on earth is so meaningful until you really talk about it

life on earth was always so sinkable, no one bought into it

life on earth is thickening in the pan

I hand ⬚s to the teller, imperfect amount after imperfect amount. ⬚s aren't money but they can come close. shapes, we call them, because there is no living thing with which a ⬚ lines up. we call something good when we don't feel like performing a comparison. we call something lit up when its conceit cannot be described. we call something impractical when it has a meaning we are not involved in. we call something dumbfounding when it is floating in thin air.

life on earth sits in a tree like a horse. I approach and hold out an apple. THIS IS NOT A GROCERY STORE, life on earth thunders. okay. I put the apple down and try a different approach. I am only seeking success, I say. life on earth examines me like a helium balloon for leaks. I am only seeking success, I repeat. life on earth looks at me like I am a funnel cake or an idea. like a party hat or a fulcrum or a lease. I try to walk backwards but instead I approach closely. I am only seeking success, I say again, loudly. at the grocery store, life on earth announces the astonishing answer.

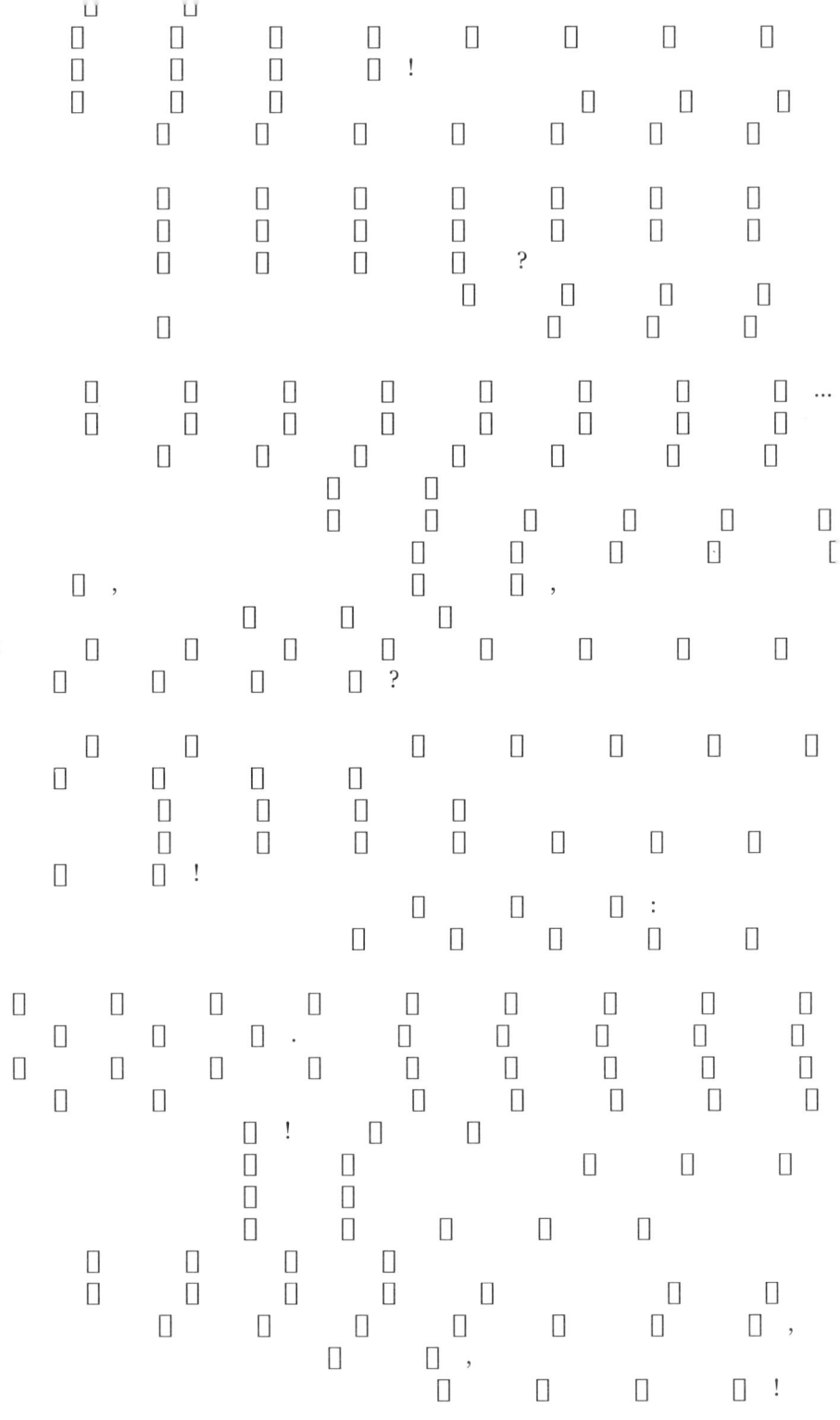

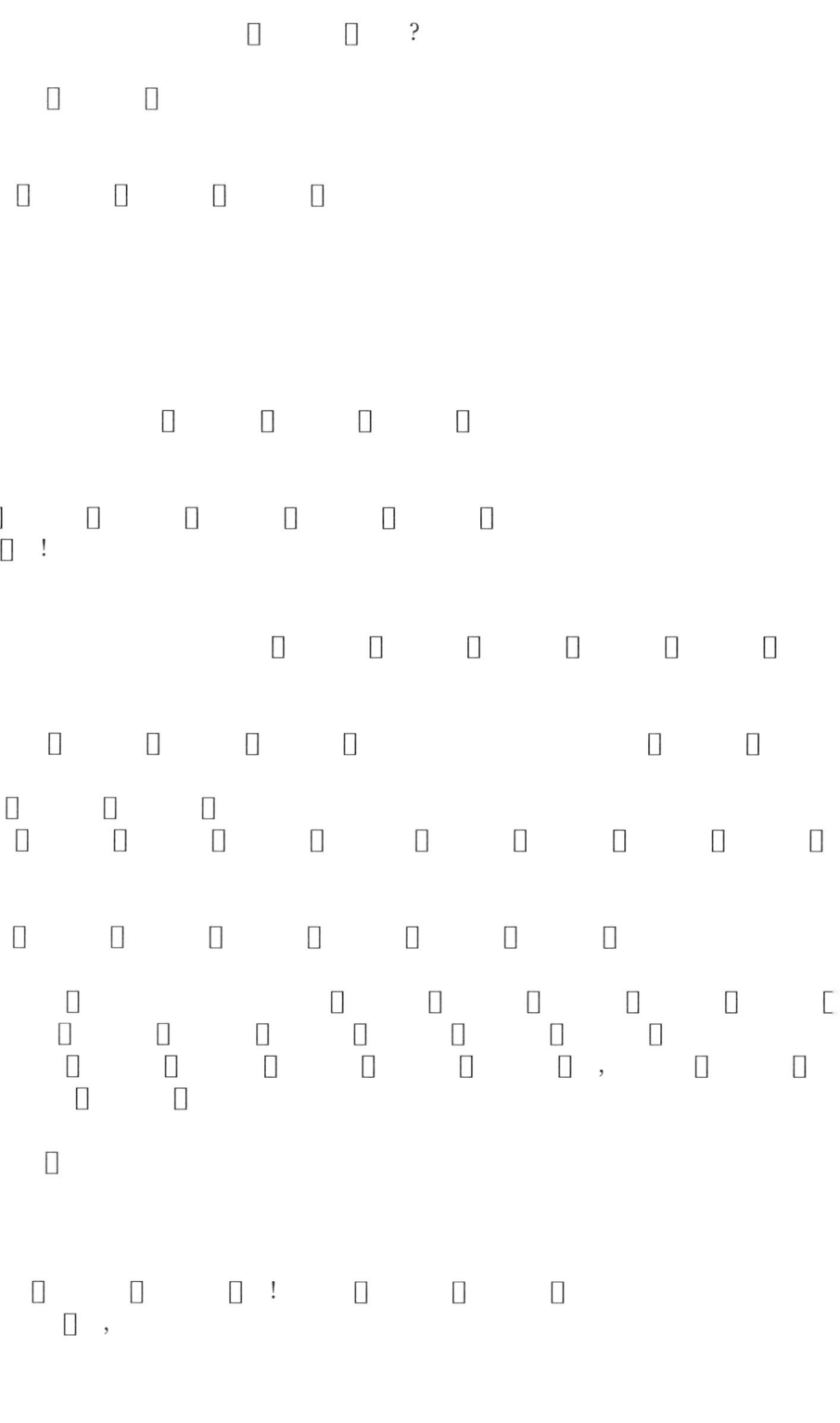

life on earth pulled from a reflecting pool a long rope attached to which was a piece of paper affixed to which was the name "life on earth" in bright and varied lights,

life on earth pulled from my eye a piece of glass made into the shape of a cloud with pointy edges and I said, thank you for doing this for me, and life on earth said, you are welcome, you are very very welcome,

life on earth pulled from out of the ground a tiny house containing a tinier apple and said without saying it, all speech is a motorcycle, soft and dangerous, and I am not going to listen to national public radio or eat beef any longer etc.,

life on earth pulled from my leg a tooth, a hostile little tooth. how do you do, life on earth said to the tooth, and the tooth who didn't know what to do, the tooth who,

life on earth pointed to a little piece of rain and said, I have no other materials from which to draw USB power, and the water on the ground became a tiny USB port to charge a tiny cellular phone, the phone said, here I am, and life on earth said, here I am, I have always wanted to come here, let me in, life on earth pointed to the "WHERE HAS ALL THE RAIN GONE" sign which contained an arrow which indicated where all the rain had gone, life on earth said, it was just here, I was sitting with it and it was all over me. then life on earth pulled my sunflower out of thin air,

I was living very simply for a long time, life on earth said. I just had a toaster oven and a toy gun that shot potatoes to my name, and then this sunflower,

it was nice to have only two things but then you made me have three, life on earth said, and then got rid of the sunflower,

life on earth pulled from the ground a kind of shape, the shape had no determined edges, it switched directions in retinal velocity, which in NASA-speak means that the shape was gigantic, it switched directions in light and wind,

is this a place you can make more places through? life on earth asked me seriously and with purpose. I nodded my many earnest heads. night was coming, whistling up from beneath the sand,

I knew we had to get ready, but where should my feet
go, how high should I count to get to the right amount,
where was my house, where was time, what was correct
to tell on social media and when would I have to wait,

I thought in all of my listening I might have moved it. I
stood very still against the loosening light,

all constant, all night, all now,

I said to the violet flower

having eaten cotton fibers

out the window ribbons and log flumes

in the windows I do research

everyone having a ticket

the accident having ended

having rode the electric airplane

the place getting ahead of me

going backwards I mean

or starting to lose detail

I caught a tremendous light-up tree

I know I can speak to  []

let me try it

I said to the violet

but the units converging

I went to the home of an upward angle. the upward angle lived in the suburbs in a house shaped like a ☐ with a triangle on top, in other words it was a regular house, a relaxed house,

life on earth said I shouldn't stop making shapes until long after the table has carried me,

so I walked inside the ☐ house, my heels on fire,
"tell me about yourself," said the upward angle,

"well," I said, "I don't want to become a witch. I don't want to become a quail. I don't want to become a spoonful of melted plastic with acorns for eyes. or a daffodil. and you?"

the upward angle said, in a rehearsed sort of way, "I don't want to become aloof. or reprehensible. or boring. I don't want to hold the milk of light any further just to be let in."

"tell me something I need to know," I said, unimpressed.

the upward angle said, "let me ask you something about telephones. which of these statements is true?

telephones are cumbersome.

telephones are boring.

telephones are all asleep.

telephones are obsolete."

but I knew the real answer, and I knew that it hadn't been
listed, so I left the upward angle to his arithmetics.

telephones are everywhere.

I was never going to die so I had to type the ending on microsoft word and make it named "ending" so I didn't forget about it. then I went and dug a hole in a hill with a sequin. it took a long time. to begin with, the sequin didn't last. after two plunges into the dirt it started to bend. at plunge seven, it gave way completely.

I started digging with other objects I found lying around nearby. a fine-tipped sharpie served a sort of ice pick functionality. a microphone did more harm than good. a feather boa was entertaining to consider but ultimately impractical. at the end of the day the top tools for digging were, in no particular order: flip flop, ▯, toy train at the bottom of the hole it started to rain and the book was suddenly over. I don't know what there is left to expect. it rained. of course it rained, it was a book called groceries. but even though it was the end of the book I didn't actually expect the rain to come, and when it came, I didn't expect it to be so ordinary. just rain making its way over the buildings and neighborhoods, the diagonal intersections and unnamable metal structures, the subway stations and the grocery stores, the bulldozers and the scaffolding. just rain on the rubber floors of the crosstown bus, the blare of the driver naming streets on the intercom, the stable itch of umbrellas underfoot, the going light tell the truth.

okay.

I made a paper pretzel.

I took my body out of it.

I chewed it on the stairs.

I brought it back to life.

I found a home I could be found in.

I found a wire I could be called on.

I found a light switch like it.

I found the truth took too much time.

a story was much simpler to convey.

nowadays I try to move more quickly.

I know how to handle elevators and landlords and fish

slipping past me on the walk.

I sidestep everything.

I live like an afternoon always.

hatred is very ordinary. the light
on the porch of the new apartment
is too gray. there is no way to fix
this except to get different light. in
general, things that have stripes
tend to be good. in general, blue
houses tend not to be content.
if you put on a blouse be sure to
overtake it. hatred is very funny.
you wear your clothes inside out
for a while. you get heavy with the
smell of sheep and dead flowers,
or the wayside wind, or molecules.
anyway, like I told Kate on the phone,
there isn't any real way to get anger
to count these days. it seems like
in three or four ways, things just keep on
gluing past it. and I guess there would
be no place left to go, except going
is sub zero. to get to the dial pad you
have to bounce off tables and come
and go with lines. to get by on earth
you really have to ☐ it. to get started you
just have to get general, be good,
be blue, be not impertinent, be vernal
gray in a bucket of cereal, be whimsy,
be grateful, be single-handed, be clod,
be ominous like a see-thru violet

## ACKNOWLEDGMENTS

This book is for Kelly Clare. Thank you for sharing this alphabet and this life with me.

Thank you to all of my friends. Thanks especially to everyone who helped me make this Word document into Groceries: Kate Gibbel, Alyssa Moore, Bianca Messinger, Stephen Ira, Micky Bayonne, and Jules Wood. Thank you Elizabeth Willis, Tracie Morris, Mark Levine, John Murillo, and Michele Hardesty. Thank you poetry S=O=F=T=B=A=L=L team. Long live poetry. Long live softball. Thank you Peach pals. Thank you to my parents, my sister and my grandparents. Thank you Ramona.

I'm enormously grateful to Srikanth "Chicu" Reddy for believing in this work. Thank you so much to everyone at Fonograf Editions helping bring this book into the world, especially to Jeff Alessandrelli and Adie B. Steckel. Thank you Mike Corrao for the design.

Thank you to the editors of *Chicago Review*, *The Paris Review*, *FENCE*, *Washington Square Review*, *Bennington Review*, *Gigantic Sequins*, and *Prelude* for publishing early versions of these pages.

FONO
GRAꟻ

1. **Eileen Myles**—*Aloha/irish trees* (LP)

2. **Rae Armantrout**—*Conflation* (LP)

3. **Alice Notley**—*Live in Seattle* (LP)

4. **Harmony Holiday**—*The Black Saint and the Sinnerman* (LP)

5. **Susan Howe & Nathaniel Mackey**—*STRAY: A Graphic Tone* (LP)

6. **Annelyse Gelman & Jason Grier**—*About Repulsion* (EP)

7. **Joshua Beckman**—*Some Mechanical Poems To Be Read Aloud* (print)

8. **Dao Strom**—*Instrument/ Traveler's Ode* (print; cassette tape)

9. **Douglas Kearney & Val Jeanty**—*Fodder* (LP)

10. **Mark Leidner**—*Returning the Sword to the Stone* (print)

11. **Charles Valle**—*Proof of Stake: An Elegy* (print)

12. **Emily Kendal Frey**—*LOVABILITY* (print)

13. **Brian Laidlaw and the Family Trade**—*THIS ASTER: adaptations of Emile Nelligan* (LP)

14. **Nathaniel Mackey and The Creaking Breeze Ensemble**—*Fugitive Equation* (compact disc)

15. *FE Magazine* (print)

16. **Brandi Katherine Herrera**—*MOTHER IS A BODY* (print)

17. **Jan Verberkmoes**—*Firewatch* (print)

18. **Krystal Languell**—*Systems Thinking with Flowers* (print)

19. **Matvei Yankelevich**—*Dead Winter* (print)

20. **Cody-Rose Clevidence**—*Dearth & God's Green Mirth* (print)

21. **Hilary Plum**—*Hole Studies* (print)

22. **John Ashbery**—*Live at Sanders Theatre, 1976* (LP)

23. **Alice Notley**—*The Speak Angel Series* (print)

24. **Alice Notley**—*Early Works* (print)

25. **Joshua Marie Wilkinson**—*Trouble Finds You* (print)

26. **Timmy Straw**—*The Thomas Salto* (print)

27. **Audre Lorde**—*At Fassett Studio, 1970* (LP)

28. **Gabriel Palacios**—*A Ten Peso Burial For Which Truth I Sign* (print)

29. **Isabel Zapata, trans. Robin Myers**—*A Whale Is a Country* (print)

30. **Callum Angus**—*Cataract* (print)

31. *FE/De-Canon Anthology* (print)

32. **Cody-Rose Clevidence**—*The Grimace of Eden, Now* (print)

33. **Jaydra Johnson**—*Low: Notes on Art and Trash* (print)

34. **Jaime Gil de Biedma**—*If Only For a Moment (I'll Never Be Young Again)* (print)

35. **Esther Kondo Heller**—*AR:RANGE:MENTS* (print)

36. **Ahmad Almallah**—*Wrong Winds* (print)

37. **Kimberly Alidio**—*Traceable Relation* (print)

38. **Sara Gilmore**—*The Green Lives* (print)

39. **Darcie Dennigan**—*Little Neck* (print)

Fonograf Editions is a registered 501(c)(3) nonprofit organization. Find more information about the press at: fonografeditions.com.